The poems in *There's Always Pooh and Me* are taken from
When We Were Very Young (originally published in Great Britain 6 November 1924)
and *Now We Are Six* (originally published in Great Britain 13 October 1927)
by Methuen & Co. Ltd.
Text by A.A. Milne and line illustrations by Ernest H. Shepard
copyright under the Berne Convention.

This edition published in Great Britain 2002
by Egmont Books Limited
239 Kensington High Street
London W8 6SA.

1 3 5 7 9 10 8 6 4 2

ISBN 0 4162 0036 2

Printed in China

Wherever I Am, There's Always Pooh

There's Always Pooh and Me

A Collection of Poems
by A.A.MILNE

Illustrated by E.H.Shepard

Over seventy-five years ago . . .

A.A Milne wrote these poems for his small son Christopher Robin.

CONTENTS

THE CHRISTENING

What shall I call
   My dear little dormouse?
His eyes are small,
   But his tail is e-nor-mouse.

I sometimes call him Terrible John,

'Cos his tail goes on – And on – And on.

And I sometimes call him Terrible Jack,
'Cos his tail goes on to the end of his back.
And I sometimes call him Terrible James,
'Cos he says he likes me calling him names. . . .

But I think I shall call him Jim,
'Cos *I am* fond of him.

FURRY BEAR

If I were a bear,
   And a big bear too,
I shouldn't much care
   If it froze or snew;
I shouldn't much mind
   If it snowed or friz –
I'd be all fur-lined
   With a coat like his!

For I'd have fur boots and a brown fur wrap,
And brown fur knickers and a big fur cap.
I'd have a fur muffle-ruff to cover my jaws,
And brown fur mittens on my big brown paws.
With a big brown furry-down up to my head,
I'd sleep all the winter in a big fur bed.

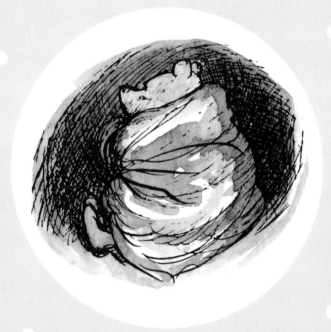

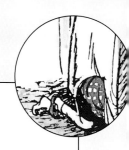

MISSING

Has anybody seen my mouse?

I opened his box for half a minute,
Just to make sure he was really in it,
And while I was looking, he jumped outside!
I tried to catch him, I tried, I tried. . . .
I think he's somewhere about the house.
Has *anyone* seen my mouse?

Uncle John, have you seen my mouse?

Just a small sort of mouse, a dear little brown one,
He came from the country, he wasn't a town one,
So he'll feel all lonely in a London street;
Why, what could he possibly find to eat?

He must be somewhere. I'll ask Aunt Rose:
Have *you* seen a mouse with a woffelly nose?
Oh, somewhere about –
He's just got out . . .

Hasn't *anybody* seen my mouse?

FORGIVEN

I found a little beetle, so that Beetle was his name,
And I called him Alexander and he answered just the same.
I put him in a match-box, and I kept him all the day . . .
And Nanny let my beetle out –

Yes, Nanny let my beetle out –

She went and let my beetle out –

And Beetle ran away.

She said she didn't mean it, and I never said she did,
She said she wanted matches and she just took off the lid,
She said that she was sorry, but it's difficult to catch
An excited sort of beetle you've mistaken for a match.

She said that she was sorry, and I really mustn't mind,
As there's lots and lots of beetles which she's certain we
could find,

If we looked about the garden for the holes where beetles hid –

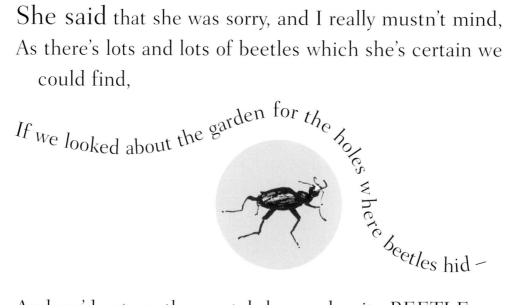

And we'd get another match-box and write BEETLE
on the lid.

We went to all the places which a beetle might be near,
And we made the sort of noises which a beetle likes to hear,
And I saw a kind of something, and I gave a sort of shout:
"A beetle-house and Alexander Beetle coming out!"

It was Alexander Beetle I'm as certain as can be,
And he had a sort of look as if he thought it must be Me,
And he had a sort of look as if he thought he ought to say:

"I'm very very sorry that I tried to run away."

And Nanny's very sorry too for you-know-what-she-did,
And she's writing **ALEXANDER** very blackly on the lid,
So Nan and me are friends, because it's difficult to catch
An excited Alexander you've mistaken for a match.

CHERRY STONES

Tinker, Tailor,

Soldier, Sailor,

Rich Man,

Poor Man,

Ploughboy,

Thief –

18

And what about a Cowboy,
Policeman, Jailer,
Engine-driver,
Or Pirate Chief?
What about a Postman – or a Keeper at the Zoo?
What about the Circus Man who lets the people through?
And the man who takes the pennies for the roundabouts and
  swings?
Or the man who plays the organ, and the other man who
  sings?
What about a Conjuror with rabbits in his pockets?
What about a Rocket Man who's always making rockets?
Oh, there's such a lot of things to do and such a lot to be
That there's always lots of cherries on my little cherry tree!

THE ENGINEER

Let it rain!
Who cares?
I've a train

Upstairs,

With a brake
Which I make
From a string
Sort of thing,
Which works
In jerks,
'Cos it drops
In the spring,
Which stops
With the string,

And the wheels
All stick
So quick
That is feels
Like a thing
That you make
With a brake,
Not string. . . .

So that's what I make,
When the day's all wet.
It's a good sort of brake
But it hasn't worked yet.

WAITING AT THE WINDOW

These are my two drops of rain
Waiting on the window-pane.

I am waiting here to see
Which the winning one will be.

Both of them have different names.
One is John and one is James.

All the best and all the worst
Comes from which of them is first.

James has just begun to ooze.
He's the one I want to lose.

John is waiting to begin.
He's the one I want to win.

James is going slowly on.
Something sort of sticks to John.

John is moving off at last.
James is going pretty fast.

John is rushing down the pane.
James is going slow again.

James has met a sort of smear.
John is getting very near.

Is he going fast enough?
(James has found a piece of fluff.)

John has hurried quickly by.
(James was talking to a fly.)

John is there, and John has won!
Look! I told you! Here's the sun!

IN THE FASHION

A lion has a tail and a very fine tail,
And so has an elephant, and so has a whale,
And so has a crocodile, and so has a quail –
   They've all got tails but me.

If I had sixpence I would buy one;
I'd say to the shopman, "Let me try one";
I'd say to the elephant, "This is *my* one."
   They'd all come round to see.

Then I'd say to the lion, "Why, *you've* got a tail!
And so has the elephant, and so has the whale!
And, look! There's a crocodile! *He's* got a tail!
   You've all got tails like me!"

NURSERY CHAIRS

One of the chairs is South America,
One of the chairs is a ship at sea,
One is a cage for a great big lion,
And one is a chair for Me.

The First Chair

When I go up the Amazon,
I stop at night and fire a gun
  To call my faithful band.
And Indians in twos and threes,
Come silently between the trees,
  And wait for me to land.
And if I do not want to play
With any Indians today,
  I simply wave my hand.
And then they turn and go away –
  They always understand.

The Second Chair

I'm a great big lion in my cage,
And I often frighten Nanny with a roar.
Then I hold her very tight, and
Tell her not to be so frightened —
And she doesn't be so frightened any more.

The Third Chair

When I am in my ship, I see
The other ships go sailing by.
A sailor leans and calls to me
As his tall ship goes sailing by.
Across the sea he leans to me,
Above the wind I hear him cry:
"Is this the way to Round-the-World?"
He calls as he goes by.

The Fourth Chair

Whenever I sit in a high chair
   For breakfast or dinner or tea,
I try to pretend that it's *my* chair,
   And that I am a baby of three.

Shall I go off to South America?
   Shall I put out in my ship to sea?
Or get in my cage and be lions and tigers?
Or – shall I be only Me?

THE FRIEND

There are lots and lots of people who are always asking
    things,
Like Dates and Pounds-and-ounces and the names of funny
    Kings,
And the answer's either Sixpence or A Hundred Inches
    Long.
And I know they'll think me silly if I get the answer wrong.

So Pooh and I go whispering, and Pooh looks very bright,
 And says, "Well, *I* say sixpence, but I don't suppose I'm
    right."
And then it doesn't matter what the answer ought to be,
'Cos if he's right, I'm Right, and if he's wrong, it isn't Me.

KNIGHT-IN-ARMOUR

Whenever I'm a shining Knight,
I buckle on my armour tight;
And then I look about for things,
Like Rushings-Out, and Rescuings,
And Savings from the Dragon's Lair,
And fighting all the Dragons there.
And sometimes when our fights begin,
I think I'll let the Dragons win . . .
And then I think perhaps I won't,
Because they're Dragons, and I don't.

BAD SIR BRIAN BOTANY

Sir Brian had a battleaxe with great big knobs on;
   He went among the villagers and blipped them on the
      head.
On Wednesday and on Saturday, but mostly on the latter
      day,
   He called at all the cottages, and this is what he said:

   "I am Sir Brian!" *(ting-ling)*

    "I am Sir Brian!" *(rat-tat)*

   "I am Sir Brian, as bold as a lion –

     Take *that!* – and *that!* – and *that!*"

Sir Brian had a pair of boots with great big spurs on,
    A fighting pair of which he was particularly fond.
On Tuesday and on Friday, just to make the street look tidy,
    He'd collect the passing villagers and kick them in the
        pond.

"I am Sir Brian!" *(sper-lash!)*

"I am Sir Brian!" *(sper-losh!)*

"I am Sir Brian, as bold as a lion –

Is anyone else for a wash?"

Sir Brian woke one morning, and he couldn't find his
    battleaxe;
He walked into the village in his second pair of boots.
He had gone a hundred paces, when the street was full of
    faces,
And the villagers were round him with ironical salutes.

"You are Sir Brian? Indeed!

You are Sir Brian? Dear, dear!

You are Sir Brian, as bold as a lion?

Delighted to meet you here!"

Sir Brian went a journey, and he found a lot of duckweed;

They pulled him out and dried him, and they blipped him
on the head.
They took him by the breeches, and they hurled him into
ditches,
And they pushed him under waterfalls, and this is what
they said:

"You are Sir Brian – don't laugh,

You are Sir Brian – don't cry;

You are Sir Brian, as bold as a lion –

Sir Brian, the lion, good-bye!"

Sir Brian struggled home again, and chopped up his battleaxe,
  Sir Brian took his fighting boots, and threw them in the
      fire.
He is quite a different person now he hasn't got his spurs on,
  And he goes about the village as B. Botany, Esquire.

"I am Sir Brian? Oh, *no*!

I am Sir Brian? Who's he?

I haven't got any title, I'm Botany –

Plain Mr Botany (B)."

BUCKINGHAM PALACE

They're changing guard at Buckingham Palace –
Christopher Robin went down with Alice.
Alice is marrying one of the guard.
"A soldier's life is terrible hard,"

                                        Says Alice.

They're changing guard at Buckingham Palace –
Christopher Robin went down with Alice.
We saw a guard in a sentry-box.
"One of the sergeants looks after their socks,"

                                        Says Alice.

They're changing guard at Buckingham Palace –
Christopher Robin went down with Alice.
We looked for the King, but he never came.
"Well, God take care of him, all the same,"

Says Alice.

They're changing guard at Buckingham Palace –
Christopher Robin went down with Alice.
They've great big parties inside the grounds.
"I wouldn't be King for a hundred pounds,"

Says Alice.

They're changing guard at Buckingham Palace –
Christopher Robin went down with Alice.
A face looked out, but it wasn't the King's.
"He's much too busy a-signing things,"

Says Alice.

They're changing guard at Buckingham Palace –
Christopher Robin went down with Alice.
"Do you think the King knows all about *me*?"
"Sure to, dear, but it's time for tea,"

Says Alice.

THE KING'S BREAKFAST

The King asked
The Queen, and
The Queen asked
The Dairymaid:
"Could we have some butter for
The Royal slice of bread?"
The Queen asked
The Dairymaid,
The Dairymaid
Said, "Certainly,
I'll go and tell
The cow
Now
Before she goes to bed."

The Dairymaid
She curtsied,

And went and told
The Alderney:
"Don't forget the butter for
The Royal slice of bread."

The Alderney
Said sleepily:
"You'd better tell
His Majesty
That many people nowadays
Like marmalade
Instead."

The Dairymaid
Said, "Fancy!"
And went to
Her Majesty.
She curtsied to the Queen, and
She turned a little red:
"Excuse me,
Your Majesty,
For taking of
The liberty,
But marmalade is tasty, if
It's very
Thickly
Spread."

The Queen said,
"Oh!"
And went to
His Majesty:
"Talking of the butter for
The Royal slice of bread,
Many people
Think that
Marmalade
Is nicer.
Would you like to try a little
Marmalade
Instead?"

The King said,
"Bother!"
And then he said,
"Oh, deary me!"
The King sobbed,
"Oh, deary me!"
And went back to bed.
"Nobody,"
He whimpered,
"Could call me
A fussy man;
I *only* want
A little bit
Of butter for
My bread!"

The Queen said,
"There, there!"
And went to
The Dairymaid.
The Dairymaid
Said, "There, there!"
And went to the shed.
The cow said,
"There, there!
I didn't really
Mean it;
Here's milk for his porringer.
And butter for his bread."

The Queen took
The butter
And brought it to
His Majesty;
The King said,
"Butter, eh?"
And bounced out of bed.
"Nobody," he said,
As he kissed her
Tenderly,

"Nobody," he said,
As he slid down
The banisters,
"Nobody,
My darling,
Could call me
A fussy man –
BUT

I do like a little bit of butter to my bread!"

KNIGHTS AND LADIES

There is in my old picture book
A page at which I like to look,
Where knights and squires come riding down
The cobbles of some steep old town,
And ladies from beneath the eaves
Flutter their bravest handkerchiefs,
Or, smiling proudly, toss down gages . . .
But that was in the Middle Ages.
It wouldn't happen now; but still,
Whenever I look up the hill
Where, dark against the green and blue,
The firs come marching, two by two,
I wonder if perhaps I *might*
See suddenly a shining knight
Winding his way from blue to green –
Exactly as it would have been
Those many, many years ago. . . .
Perhaps I might. You never know.

JOURNEY'S END

Christopher, Christopher, where are you going,

Christopher Robin?

"Just up to the top of the hill,
Upping and upping until
I am right on the top of the hill,"

Said Christopher Robin.

Christopher, Christopher, why are you going,

Christopher Robin?

*There's nothing to see, so when
You've got to the top, what then?*

"Just down to the bottom again,"

Said Christopher Robin.

THE ISLAND

If I had a ship,
I'd sail my ship,
I'd sail my ship
Through Eastern seas;
Down to a beach where the slow waves thunder—
The green curls over and the white falls under—

Boom! Boom! Boom!
On the sun-bright sand.
Then I'd leave my ship and I'd land,
And climb the steep white sand,
And climb to the trees,
The six dark trees,
The coco-nut trees on the cliff's green crown —
Hands and knees
To the coco-nut trees,
Face to the cliff as the stones patter down,

Up, up, up, staggering, stumbling,
Round the corner where the rock is crumbling,
Round this shoulder,
Over this boulder,
Up to the top where the six trees stand. . . .

And there would I rest, and lie,
My chin in my hands, and gaze
At the dazzle of sand below,
And the green waves curling slow,
And the grey-blue distant haze
Where the sea goes up to the sky. . . .

And I'd say to myself as I looked so lazily down at the sea:
"There's nobody else in the world, and the world was made
   for me."

SNEEZLES

Christopher Robin
Had wheezles
And sneezles,
They bundled him
Into
His bed.
They gave him what goes
With a cold in the nose,
And some more for a cold
In the head.
They wondered
If wheezles
Could turn
Into measles,
If sneezles
Would turn
Into mumps;
They examined his chest
For a rash,
And the rest
Of his body for swellings and lumps.

They sent for some doctors
In sneezles
And wheezles
To tell them what ought
To be done.

All sorts and conditions
Of famous physicians
Came hurrying round
At a run.

They all made a note
Of the state of his throat,
They asked if he suffered from thirst;
They asked if the sneezles
Came *after* the wheezles,
Or if the first sneezle
Came first.
They said, "If you teazle
A sneezle
Or wheezle,
A measle
May easily grow.
But humour or pleazle
The wheezle
Or sneezle,
The measle
Will certainly go."

They expounded the reazles
For sneezles
And wheezles
The manner of measles
When new.
They said "If he freezles
In draughts and breezles,
Then PHTHEEZLES
May even ensue."

.   .   .   .

Christopher Robin
Got up in the morning,
The sneezles had vanished away.
And the look in his eye
Seemed to say to the sky,
"*Now, how to amuse them to-day?*"

SOLITUDE

I have a house where I go
   When there's too many people,
I have a house where I go
   Where no one can be;
I have a house where I go,
Where nobody ever says "No"
Where no one says anything – so
   There is no one but me.

HAPPINESS

John had
Great Big
Waterproof
Boots on;
John had a
Great Big
Waterproof
Hat;
John had a
Great Big
Waterproof
Mackintosh –
And that
(Said John)
   Is
   That.

SPRING MORNING

Where am I going? I don't quite know.
Down to the stream where the king-cups grow –
Up to the hill where the pine-trees blow –
Anywhere, anywhere. *I* don't know.

Where am I going? The clouds sail by,
Little ones, baby ones, over the sky.
Where am I going? The shadows pass,
Little ones, baby ones, over the grass.

If you were a cloud, and sailed up there,
You'd sail on water as blue as air,
And you'd see me here in the fields and say:
"Doesn't the sky look green to-day?"

Where am I going? The high rooks call:
"It's awful fun to be born at all."
Where am I going? The ring-doves coo:
"We do have beautiful things to do."

If you were a bird, and lived on high,
You'd lean on the wind when the wind came by,
You'd say to the wind when it took you away:
"*That's* where I wanted to go to-day!"

Where am I going? I don't quite know.
What does it matter where people go?
Down to the wood where the blue-bells grow –
Anywhere, anywhere. *I* don't know.

JONATHAN JO

Jonathan Jo
Has a mouth like an "O"
And a wheelbarrow full of surprises;
If you ask for a bat,
Or for something like that,
He has got it, whatever the size is.

If you're wanting a ball,
It's no trouble at all;
Why, the more that you ask for, the merrier –
Like a hoop and a top,
And a watch that won't stop,
And some sweets, and an Aberdeen terrier.

Jonathan Jo
Has a mouth like an "O,"
But this is what makes him so funny
If you give him a smile,
Only once in a while,
Then he never expects any money!

US TWO

Wherever I am, there's always Pooh,
There's always Pooh and Me.
Whatever I do, he wants to do,
"Where are you going to-day?" says Pooh:
"Well, that's very odd 'cos I was too.
Let's go together," says Pooh, says he.
"Let's go together," says Pooh.

"What's twice eleven?" I said to Pooh,
("Twice what?" said Pooh to Me.)
"*I think* it ought to be twenty-two."
"Just what I think myself," said Pooh.
"It wasn't an easy sum to do,
But that's what it is," said Pooh, said he.
"That's what it is," said Pooh.

"Let's look for dragons," I said to Pooh.
"Yes, let's," said Pooh to Me.
We crossed the river and found a few –
"Yes, those are dragons all right," said Pooh.
"As soon as I saw their beaks I knew.
That's what they are," said Pooh, said he.
"That's what they are," said Pooh.

"Let's frighten the dragons," I said to Pooh.
"That's right," said Pooh to Me.
"*I'm* not afraid," I said to Pooh,
And I held his paw and shouted "Shoo!
Silly old dragons!" – and off they flew.
"I wasn't afraid," said Pooh, said he,
"I'm *never* afraid with you."

So wherever I am, there's always Pooh,
There's always Pooh and Me.
"What would I do?" I said to Pooh,
"If it wasn't for you," and Pooh said: "True,
It isn't much fun for One, but Two
Can stick together," says Pooh, says he.
"That's how it is," says Pooh.